A

PROGRESSIVE

EDUCATION

TURTLE POINT PRESS NEW YORK 2014

A

PROGRESSIVE

EDUCATION

RICHARD

HOWARD

PUBLISHED BY TURTLE POINT PRESS

WWW.TURTLEPOINTPRESS.COM

COPYRIGHT © 2014 BY RICHARD HOWARD

ALL RIGHTS RESERVED

ISBN 978-1-933527-82-6

LCCN 2013935146

PRINTED ON ACID-FREE, RECYCLED PAPER

IN THE UNITED STATES OF AMERICA

FOR
ANNE LOESSER HOLLANDER
WHO, FOLLOWING ME
(ONE YEAR BEHIND)
HAS SHARED WITH ME
OUR PARK SCHOOL LIVES
EVER SINCE

CONTENTS

A

PROGRESSIVE

EDUCATION

OUR SPRING TRIP

Dear Mrs. Masters, Hi! from the Sixth Grade Class
of Park School! We're still here in New York City
                    at the Taft Hotel,
as you must have guessed from the picture printed
on this stationery—we inked in X's
            to show you our rooms
which are actually on the same floor as
the Terminal Tower Observation Deck
                    in Cleveland, Ohio
which we visited on our *Fifth Grade Spring Trip*,
but nowhere near so high as some skyscrapers
            in New York City:
we've been up to the *top* of the Empire State
and the Chrysler Buildings, which are really *high*!
                    But there's another
reason to write besides wanting to say Hi!
We're having a dilemma Miss Husband thought
            you might help us solve
once we get back to school . . . Yesterday we went

to that Dinosaur Hall of the Natural
                    History Museum
for our Class Project—as you know, the Sixth Grade
is constructing a life-size Diplodocus
          out of chicken-wire
and stuff that Miss Husband calls *papier-mâché*,
but no instructions seem to show how the tail
                    balances the head
to keep our big guy upright. We need to see
how the backbone of a real Diplodocus
          (it doesn't even
need to be a live one, we could probably
figure all this out from a good skeleton)
                    manages to bear
so much weight—did you know that some Dinosaurs
(like the Brontosaurus) are so huge they have
          a whole other brain
at the base of their spine just to move their tail?
Another thing: each time Arthur Engelhurst
                    comes anywhere near
our Diplodocus, it collapses because
of not balancing right. This went on until

David Stackover

got so mad at Arthur he assaulted him

in the boys' cloak-room and gave his left shoulder

a really good bite—

David claimed it seemed like the one thing which could

keep Arthur away . . . And that was the moment

you claimed the best thing

to do was to call an All-School Assembly

to explain about biting. Biting's no good . . . ?

(Which was why Arthur

decided not to come on this year's Spring Trip.)

But we took a Subway train from the Hotel

to the Museum

(actually our first New York excursion),

where the uproar, once we were on the platform,

was so loud one girl

—Nancy Angrush—cried (she was always chicken)

when someone told her that terrible roaring

the Express Trains made

was Tyrannosaurus Rex himself—*and she*

believed it! Well, then we got to the Great Hall

and were surrounded

by Dinosaurs, each species we had studied:
some were not much bigger than chickens, but some
 were humongous!
One was just a skeleton wired together,
so it was easy to see how we could make
 our Diplodocus
balance by putting a swivel in its neck.
All the other dinosaurs were stuffed with lights
 and motors inside,
so that when they moved, *their* heads balanced their tails!
There was even a Pterodactyl flying
 back and forth above
our heads, probably on some kind of track . . .
But even though Miss Husband tried explaining
 (for the hundredth time)
how the Dinosaurs had all been extinct for
millions of years, not one person in the class
 believed what she said:
the idea of a million years is so *stupid*,
anyway—typical grown-up reasoning . . .
 You know the Klein twins—
the biggest brains in the whole Sixth Grade (a lot

bigger, probably, than *both* brains combined in

that Brontosaurus)—

well, they had a question for Miss Husband: What

if the Dinosaurs being extinct for so long

is just a smoke-screen

for being Somewhere Else, a long ways away?

And Lucy Wenzel made an awful pun on

stinky and *extinct* . . .

Actually, Mrs. Masters, we've already

figured it out, about death: the Dinosaurs

may be extinct, but

they're not dead! It's a different thing, you dig?

When Duncan Chu's lhasa jumped out the window,

or when Miss Husband's

parents were killed together in a car-crash,

we understood that—that was being dead; gone:

no body around.

Isn't that what dying has to mean: not being

here? The Dinosaurs are with us all the time,

anything but dead—

we keep having them! Later, at the "Diner-

Saurus" (the Museum restaurant) there was

chicken-breast for lunch

stamped out in the shape of a Triceratops!

Strange, how everything has to taste like chicken:

whether it's rabbit

or rattlesnake, it' s always "just like chicken". . . .

Anyway, Dinosaurs are alive as long

as we think they are,

not like Duncan's dog. And that's just the problem.

By next week, though, we'll be back in Sandusky,

and while we're putting

the swivel into our Diplodocus's neck

you could explain to us about Time—

those millions of years,

and Dinosaur-chicken in the Diner, and

chicken-size Dinosaurs in the Great Hall, and

where they really are.

BACK FROM OUR SPRING TRIP

Dear Mrs. Masters, Hi! all over again
from the Sixth Grade Class of Park School. We're home now
                                    from New York City,
which sure seems different from our Sandusky,
even from Cleveland, a much bigger town where
                    most of our students
live, but nothing like New York or even just
Manhattan, where first of all we found out from
                                    the Head Curator
of the Dinosaur Wing (no more than a wing!
that gives you some idea of the difference)
                    how we could balance
our model Diplodocus's neck and tail
(with a swivel, exactly the way *they* do—
                                    they even showed us!)
and now we don't need to worry any more
about Arthur Engelhurst making our
                    dinosaur collapse
whenever he comes near it. You remember

about David Stackover *biting* Arthur so

              he would keep away?

and you called a Middle School Assembly to tell

everyone that biting's no good? Only now

         Arthur's done something

really awful, so our whole class has voted

to Report to the Authorities (which means

              to you, doesn't it?)

exactly What Happened. You see, there was this

huge male peacock—a really fine specimen,

        Mr. Lee would call him:

they look great this time of year—the way their necks

glisten seems to respond to the way they spread

           their tail-feather "eyes"

(actually that's how Miss Husband described

what all of us could see for ourselves last week

        when an entire flock

of these magic birds posed and strutted for us

in the Central Park Zoo) . . . Well, one of those birds

         managed to get itself

inside the Park School parking-lot—just strayed in

through the open gate, we thought, and there was Joe,

our old janitor,
feeding him bread-crusts out of his own lunch-box,
which was easy to do because the peacock
                    had conveniently
chosen the hood of a purple Pierce-Arrow
(he was actually standing right *on* that
          chromium archer).
Mrs. Masters, did you know that someone here
in Sandusky *raises* peacocks? His name is
                    Felice Finnegan,
and he's been doing it for years—he sells them
to parks and zoos and sometimes gives them to friends:
          a woman who lives
near Park School has six or seven of his birds,
but none of them ever managed to escape
                    until this one did,
although it seemed quite tame and willing to perch
on that car hood, eating bread from the hand of
          anyone who would
feed him. Right after What Happened, someone phoned
Mr. Finnegan, who straightaway appeared
                    at the parking lot:

he told us this bird was ten years old (which is
as old as most of us) but knew no better.
                No better than what?
Joe Sanchez (that's our old parking attendant)
said he—the peacock, not Mr. Sanchez—could
                            have gone on eating
bread all day long, but then Arthur Engelhurst
(Mr. Sanchez didn't know his name of course:
                Duncan Chu told him)
came out of nowhere as if he already
heard the peacock was there on the Pierce-Arrow
                            and ran right over
and grabbed it by that beautiful neck, dragged it
down to the gravel and started kicking and
                stomping the poor bird,
which once Arthur got a hold of it began
screaming, and then Mr. Sanchez was screaming, and
                            even Arthur was
screaming, I guess. Minutes later the peacock
was so beaten up most of its tail feathers
                had fallen out, but
it wasn't dead yet, just lying on the ground

thumping its wings, trying to get away from

                                  Arthur Engelhurst.

That was when Felice Finnegan came, and he

started screaming too, but screaming at Arthur:

                    "What are you doing?

Are you nuts?" and Arthur screamed back "Can't you see?

Let me finish, this has to be done right: I'm

                          killing a vampire!"

And just then Mr. Finnegan did something

that made the peacock stop screaming and struggling—

                    I think it died then,

but by the time Felice Finnegan had called

the police—they came right away, they're always

                          around school somewhere—

Arthur was Nowhere To Be Found. However

Duncan Chu was able to give them Arthur's

                address—he lives with

some relative who looks after him, sort of.

(Duncan Chu isn't a snitch, he knows all our

                        names and addresses

the same way he knows Chinese and math—it's how

his mind works: lists and tables are just *in there*.)

Mrs. Masters, our

whole Sixth Grade Class voted unanimously

to report What Happened because we all think

Arthur Engelhurst

should be punished, maybe expelled from Park School—

we all know for a fact he doesn't even

believe in vampires,

no one in our Class does—not enough to kill

a tame ten-year-old peacock for being one.

Arthur Engelhurst

doesn't believe in anything, he just likes

destroying things—if our Diplodocus were

alive, he'd kill it!

Our whole class is convinced that dinosaurs—all

dinosaurs, not just our own Diplodocus—

are alive somewhere

on Earth, and both Lucy Wenzel and Nancy

Angrush have heard Arthur say he wants to kill

some of the big ones

wherever they are: he was warming up on

Felice Finnegan's bird. We're asking you now

to expel Arthur

and buy the peacock lady *another* bird
(not one that's already ten years old—a chick
       would be fine with us:
we could feed it bread and watch it grow). No one
in our Class, I told you, believes a peacock
                  could be a vampire,
or even really believes in vampires. So
please, Mrs. Masters, expel Arthur from school
       or at least put him
in some other Class. This request has been signed
unanimously by the entire Sixth Grade:
                 we hope to hear from you
with some substantial response along these lines . . .

WHAT THE FUTURE HAS IN STORE

FOR RIKA LESSER

Dear Mrs. Masters,
the Sixth-Grade Class of Park School herewith submits
our Research Project for the year 2000!
                              In choosing its theme
            we have attempted
to follow the guide-lines Miss Husband furnished, ·
noting first of all our Project's awesome date,
                              which appears to be
            widely regarded
as some sort of turning-point in History;
and second, Park School's official Mandate that
                              each Project must show
            some relevance to
Life As It Is Actually Lived on Earth
(a statement not likely to phase our class, or
                              any Park School Class,
            even those less well

endowed than our Sixth Graders in matters of

vocabulary. Yet each Sixth-Grade Project

                                 that we consulted

     dealt exclusively

with *Past Achievements*, so therefore, on account

of this year being Millennial, *our own*

                              Sixth-Grade Class voted

     unanimously

to concentrate on what the *Future* may have

in store for us—and how, specifically for this class,

                         our Millennial

     hopes and promises

will eventuate. What has inspired us most,

as you're about to learn, if you'll read on,

                         has been a field-trip

     our entire class made

only two weeks ago (we're still living it!)

to the Reptile House of the Cleveland Zoo. But

                     before we tell you

     whatever we learned

there at the zoo about *Life as . . . Lived on Earth,*

you should know (you probably do already:

it's a Required Course)

that our Sixth-Grade Class

has also taken this year what the Office

calls our *Hygiene Concentration* (most of us

prefer calling it

by another name),

whereby we venture to investigate those

so-called human mysteries "*which upon some*

investigations

cease," said Mr. Lee,

Park School's Science Spokesperson,

"*being mysteries at all.*" "*What a pity!*"

rejoined Miss Husband,

Park School's Idealist,

when we learned about Sexual Intercourse

between Men & Women. Some Class members claim

they knew already,

but according to

Miss Husband, most people know *different things*

about S.I., yet what Promotes Fulfillment

in Sexual Life

(her actual words)

is that everybody should know *the same things.*

Well, for us this has been what Miss Husband calls

a challenging term,

because the whole Class

finds it hard to believe that grownup people

voluntarily subject themselves to such

senseless behavior

(which Miss Husband says

they must, in order to produce children) and

even hope to gain some form of pleasure by

taking part in it!

Some girls in our Class

—Lois Hexter and Lucy Wenzel, for instance—

claim the film we were shown and the "clinical"

vocabulary

Miss Husband employed

to describe what invariably goes on

during S.I. made the whole thing seem rather

disagreeable,

to say the least, and

sometimes really disgusting. All three Davids—

Stackover, McConnahey and Hammerstein—

                refuse to believe

    that their parents, just

to have *them*, did what we all *saw* in that film—

the Davids are sure they'd have heard their parents

             complain about that.

    Dear Mrs. Masters,

perhaps now you can understand how, after

the disturbing revelations of Hygiene,

           our Class responded

    not only with real

Enthusiasm but also with something like

Hope to what amounts to an alternative

           view of a Future

    free from the horrors

of Sexual Intercourse. We gained this new

Vision on our field trip, as we were saying,

           to the Reptile House

    of the Cleveland Zoo,

which has an unusual collection of

Komodo Dragons there—the biggest lizards

           on earth, ten feet long,

dinosaurs really,
solitary creatures that associate
only for mating, which their keepers report
is so grim to see
that they now confine
each Dragon in a separate cage. Here's what
happens, according to eye-witness accounts:
first the male vomits
to prepare himself,
then he flicks his long blue tongue at the female
to judge *receptivity*; if she resists
(with her claws and teeth)
he has to pin her
to the ground during S.I. (with most livestock
it's called *covering*) to avoid getting hurt.
The keepers told us
that after S.I.
it takes a Dragon Mom seven months to hatch
her clutch of some 20 eggs, and after that
it takes five years for
young Dragons to reach
maturity—*maturity* means eating

baby Dragons (10 percent of their diet)

                which have to become

    fast tree-climbers to

avoid "predation" (a zoo expression for

not getting themselves devoured by Dragon Dads).

                We can see why zoos

    keep males apart from

females, and therefore why it must have come as

quite a surprise, two years back, for all involved

                when this one female

    went ahead and laid

a clutch of fertile eggs that managed to hatch

by a process called *parthenogenesis*—

                which means they don't *need*

    S.I. with the males.

(This also happens, one keeper informed us,

with certain fish!) Well, what we'd like to know is:

                could Science obtain

    similar results

in *humans*? If female Dragons can avoid

the discomforts and damages of S.I.

                by sheer will-power

    (that's what it *looks like*),

can't something of the kind be achieved *for us?*
Mrs. Masters, this is what our Class Project
would like to propose
as its conclusion
(with the assistance of Medical Science):
a vision of Human Life without S.I.—
a New and Improved
Version we conceived
after contemplating the likely course of
our grown-up lives in the years to come. These same
Komodo Dragons
(as we can tell from
the hatchlings' evolved stratagem of climbing
trees to escape *their own parents'* appetites)
are a high enough
form of life—higher
than "certain fish"—to provide Modern Science
a model for an ameliorated
Human Existence.
Dear Mrs. Masters,
with the single exception of Anne Wobie,
who is Catholic and therefore insists (quite
erroneously,

as it now turns out)

that there has been only One Incidence of

of parthenogenesis in *our life as*

it is lived on Earth),

the whole Sixth-Grade Class

of Park School is proud to propose this Report

on the Future Happiness of Human Life.

Perhaps one of us

in this very Class

will be able to relieve humanity

of the burden of sexual intercourse.

That is our fond hope.

(signed)

Yours Faithfully,

Judy Anders, Nancy Angrush, Duncan Chu

Arthur Engelhurst, David Hammerstein, Jane

McCullough, Lois

Hexter, Lucy Wenzel,

David McConnehey, David Stackover,

Joan Sturgess, Kenneth & Jonathan Klein,

Michael Hopkinson

ARTHUR ENGELHURST'S
BACK IN SCHOOL

Dear Mrs. Masters, as you probably know,
almost half our Sixth Grade Class is Jewish—not
      a majority
but *lots*, without even counting our teacher
Miss Husband, who's getting married (next June) to
      a *gentile husband*!
—that has to change more than her name, doesn't it?
Well, your office records must show who's really
      Jewish and who's not,
and for some of us who just *happen to be* Jewish
such records are probably the only sure
      indication of
our race or faith or whatever makes us Jews,
and therefore different from the other students
      (no one really knows).
But this week our Rabbi told us this weird thing:
he says there are Jews—mostly in Hasidic
      Congregations and

they're most frequently in Brooklyn—who between
Rosh Hashana and Yom Kippur perform a ritual
            called *pekkarot*—no,
that's backward, the Hebrew word is *kapparot*—
during which Believers swing a live chicken
                        high over their heads:
such whirling is meant to transfer the Hasid's
sins to the chicken, which is then sacrificed.
        Rabbi Abraham   ·
said about fifty thousand chickens are used
in these ceremonies all over Brooklyn—
                        that's a lot of birds
to get slaughtered (after being whirled), and most
end up in someone's pot. Not everyone whirls
        chickens, there are some
Orthodox Believers who whirl cash instead—
Maimonides himself once declared *kapparot*
                        a pagan practice
which should be abandoned, but our Rabbi says
it's going strong in Brooklyn and can't be stopped.
        Now Mrs. Masters,
we've learned—trust Duncan Chu to find out, of course—

that our Arthur Engelhurst's late parents were
                              both Hasidic Jews
(Arthur was the boy who killed that peacock, and
you wouldn't punish him, although we voted
                    unanimously
to expel him from the Sixth Grade), and when we
called on Arthur's Aunt, she showed us a photo
                              of Arthur, age six,
wearing gloves and whirling a big white rooster
for *kapparot* . . . No one knew where he had gone
                    after What Happened,
but you said we ought to help him "find himself"
if he ever came back to Park School—of course
                              the police found him
soon enough, whether Arthur had found himself
or not. Mrs. Masters, the police never
                    do much in the way
of helping lost people find themselves, even if
they're pretty good about finding missing folks,
                              especially when
they're dead. And many of us think that Arthur
believed he had to slaughter that poor peacock

for his *kapparot*—
of course he mixed it up with vampire movies
and that's what Arthur meant when he kept screaming
he had to do it

right. Nancy Angrush says religions are like
that: when everyone's forgotten what they mean,
we do what people
have always seem to have done. But we forget
parts of what's supposed to be done. Or we change.
And Nancy Angrush's
not Jewish! And then Duncan Chu said something
amazing. He said religions die once they're
proved true. So that
science is the tombstone of dead religions.
Duncan's not Jewish, but David Stackover is,
so he had to say
what his father thinks. Mr. Stackover thinks
Scientists now say the same thing as Rabbis,
without capitals.
Arthur Engelhurst ignored what everyone
was saying. He sat still and looked at the floor.

Now, though, most of us
want Arthur back in Sixth Grade—isn't that where
you said you had wanted Arthur Engelhurst
to be all along?

A SIXTH-GRADE PROTEST

Dear Mrs. Masters,
at the beginning of the School Year you said
we could tell—no, you said we *should* tell you if
anything happened
in Class that made us feel bad. Well, now it has:
two times! So we're telling. You know Mr. Lee,
our Science Teacher—
he told us: call me Dinny! We don't even
know what his real first name is, but all of us
like calling him that:
no other teacher lets us use a nickname
the way we do with each other—it doesn't
mean anything but
knowing who he is. Well, Dinny's a teacher
who likes inviting guests to his Class, people
who show us things and
let us pass them around from hand to hand—things
we've never seen before, like wild animals
from the jungle, or

baby animals that can't leave their mothers

for more than a short time . . . Well, just last April

this Mr. Schwartz came,

he's a pig-farmer and he brought a piglet

with him, for just an hour: then it had to go

back to its litter,

but we could each hold it for a few minutes.

It was an albino, which means it was all white,

except for its eyes—

pink under its long eye-lashes. But trouble

began when the piglet squealed because

Duncan Chu held it

too tight, thereby receiving a nice lapful

of soggy pellets in revenge. By that time

our whole Sixth-Grade Class

was getting a little bit worried about

the piglet's being kept too long from its sow

(that's the mother pig),

so Mr. Schwartz gave it some milk and put it

back in its black (pigskin!) bag and took it home.

That was the first time

we got upset—the whole Class: you see, next day

Dinny told us that as soon as Mr. Schwartz
                         put his piglet back
in its pen, the mother pig ate it right there
while she was nursing the rest of her litter!
               How could she do that?
Dinny tried explaining to us that the sow
hadn't realized her piglet was gone, but
                    she found something wrong
with it once it was back (because each of us
had held it), and that's when Jane McCullough and
            Nancy Angrush and
Joan Surgess started crying when Duncan Chu
insisted we should all have been wearing gloves—
                and from that point on
we all got really upset. Mrs. Masters,
we don't want sows to eat their own piglets just
          for a visit to
the Sixth Grade Class of Park School! And the next thing
that happened was even worse. Much worse! You see,
            Dinny invited
this man he knows, Mr. Van Allmen, to bring
his fourteen-foot reticulated python

to our Science Class

so we could discover for ourselves that snakes

are not slimy at all, but clean and friendly;

                he told us they make

very good pets actually, always being

"tractable" if they had had enough to eat.

        He asked volunteers

to hold "Rajah" (an appropriate name for

an Indian python, everyone agreed

                except for Arthur

Engelhurst, who kept on calling him "Roger"),

but out of the whole Class only Duncan Chu

         and the Klein twins (and

Dinny, of course) would let Mr. Van Allmen,

once he had pulled the python out of his cage,

                drape Rajah around

their shoulders the way Mr. Van Allmen did.

That was a really exciting (even if

         rather scary) class—

we learned a lot about what pythons eat, how

they hatch out of eggs, and how they live longer,

                many years longer

than human beings do, unless they're slaughtered
for their beautiful—and exorbitant—skins.

       That class was last week,
but today Dinny told us Rajah's owner
was found crushed to death in his own back-yard shed
                  near Lanesville, about
fifteen miles west of Sandusky. Medical
examiners said "death was consistent with
        asphyxiation
produced by compression of the neck and chest."
It appears Ohio law does not restrict
              ownership of snakes:
Rajah was returned to . . . Van Allmen's household.
Mrs. Masters, how could they take that killer?
       How could we accept
any more such visitors? any more such
visits? Couldn't Dinny teach us about Nature
            without our having
to learn that mother pigs eat their piglets, and
that pythons have to kill their owners, even
        when they have enough
to eat? As members of the Sixth Grade Class of

Park School, we protest against such instruction;

                            we're asking to learn

less about death and more about life—that is

what Biology's meant to mean, isn't it?

               Please try to arrange

for Dinny not to invite such guests in the

future. Most of us honestly don't believe

                         the Class can take it.

MRS. HAMMERSTEIN, A PROGRESSIVE MOTHER INDEED, VISITS PARK SCHOOL FOR THE DAY

Sorry I'm late, I had to drive *way* out of my
way to pick up coyote piss—
for the garden. We use about a quart a month:
it really does deter the deer.

This man I know at the zoo keeps it for me, for
a group of us, actually:
all gardeners. He happens to *be* a keeper—
of coyotes, hyenas, wolves,

whatever—and he keeps coyote piss as well
(yes, under refrigeration)
sells it right there at the zoo. I hate the long drive,
but I love having no more deer

in the garden. Expensive, too, or should I say
dear, but it's definitely not

a competitive item—where else can you get
coyote piss that's full strength,

not reconstituted from crystals or some kind
of concentrate? It has to be
fresh—from the wild—or the damn deer just ignore it.
I wonder how such merchandise

would be gathered? My son David says there's this thing
known as a Texas Catheter,
really nothing much more than a perforated
condom attached to a bottle . . .

Have you ever seen such goings-on at a *zoo*?
Well, neither have I—but of course
I wasn't looking . . . Who would be, unless you *knew* . . . ?
Well, however he collects it,

it works! Today our keeper told me *human hair*
has the same effect, on most deer—
we could try that. Think how much cheaper, for one thing:
a year's sweepings from the barber

would cost less than a week's gasoline! Even so,
people's hair . . . ! Better the other:
I wonder which creatures would keep off if we tried
our own instead of coyotes'?

moose? dik-dik? gazelle? caribou? gnu?

A PROPOSED CURRICULUM CHANGE

Dear Mrs. Masters,

It's happened *again*!

and the whole Sixth-Grade Class is upset
(which is why we're *writing* again: you told us
to tell you when "*anything* linked to
school" upsets the class,

so now we're telling).

You see, just last week,
thanks to Mr. Lee's

connections (that's what he calls the friends
who do him favors), our Sixth-Grade Science Class,
all twelve, until the Klein twins got mumps
—together, of course—

and had to stay home,
so we invited
Mike Rahn and Clark Teft,
the two smartest kids in the Fifth-Grade,
to come instead, since Mr. Lee specified
there would be twelve students visiting

the Sandusky Labs

                for our winter-term

                Science Field Trip, and

no one wants to see

      two favors go to waste. Dinny—that's

Mr. Lee: he *asked* our class to call him that,

      and now he's the one teacher at school

we're on first-name, or

                maybe we should say

                we're on nick-name terms

with . . . whom. Anyway,

      Dinny has this friend Dr Morton

in the Labs who told us right away: "Call me

      Mort, everyone does". Sinister, no?

Mort also told us

                about cancerous

                tumors he's growing

in mice (*inducing*

      is the term he used); when he offered

to show us results of his experiment

      there was dead silence (so to speak) till

Lucy Wenzel asked

Mort if he could tell
one mouse from the next:
"Do you ever see
individuality in mice?
You know what I mean—some particular mouse
you happen to feel like working on?"
Lucy sometimes brings
her pet guinea-pig
to school with her, so
of course she would ask
something like that. Her question surprised
"Dr Mort", but maybe what he said really
was a good answer; after a pause
he told this story:
Last week he had had
to kill a female
mouse that had produced
her first litter, and to save her young,
Mort switched them to another mouse that had just
had a first litter, to bring them up
with her own; and when

that experiment
went so well, he gave
the foster-mother
another litter of newborns just
to see what she would do. And at first it seemed
everything went well: the new babies
were fat and growing
mouse-fur already,
but then, late one night,
that foster-mother
ate them all! . . . Not only Lucy but
our whole Class, even those two poor Fifth-Graders,
listened without saying a word and
not blinking an eye.
And that was when Mort
opened the Lab door:
"All right, Boys and Girls,
please come with me now". That broke the spell,
but no one, Mrs. Masters, has ever, ever
forgotten Mort's awful narrative.
Over and over

in Dinny's classes
we've learned the lesson
Mort's lab first spelled out:
in the Animal World—and aren't we
animals too?—mothers *and* fathers always
consume their own young, regardless of
age or shape or size—

pigs in model farms,
Komodo dragons,
and now even mice!
Maybe our own parents will eat *us*
sooner or later—maybe they've eaten us
already, and the rest of *our* lives
is just the process

of *their* digestion.
That's not our life, it's
our education,
but it seems so . . . well, so one-sided!
Maybe in Seventh Grade, we'll learn things work out
the other way around, so that sons
murder their fathers,

babies eat their moms,

and Snow White becomes

her vile step-mother.

So far that's the best reason we've heard

for leaving our dear Sixth Grade behind, whether

we want to or not. Still, we don't see

why Science—even

if it's just Dinny's

show—has to be so . . .

animalistic.

That may be how Family Life is,

but in that case we'd like to put in a word

—or two—for Other Things we could be

learning *this minute.*

Duncan Chu claims the

best designation

for what we crave is

human interest: we long to learn

at Park School—or elsewhere if necessary—

how some people manage (or how they

might manage) to

keep from Behaving
like animals, not
just Becoming them.
    Is all Science a history of death?
Maybe we'll learn in Seventh Grade that no Fate
    is worse than Death after all, and that
Life will be . . . our Fate.

            Dear Mrs. Masters,
            if these suggestions
make sense to you, please
    let us (and Dinny Lee) know about
the right Courses we should take next year along
    the lines we have indicated here
and the kind of Books
            we should be reading
            over the summer . . .

(signed) Respectfully,

    the Sixth-Grade Class of Park School:

Judy Anders

Duncan Chu

Jeunesse Ames

David McConnehey

Joan Sturgess

David Stackover

Anne Wobie

Lois Hexter

Nancy Angrush

David Hammerstein

and today's guests visiting from the Fifth Grade

Michael Rahn & Clark Teft

A REPORT, FOLLOWED BY
A REMONSTRANCE

Dear Mrs. Eynon, we'd like,
first of all, to thank you for conducting
   our entire Thursday art class
on its Spring Trip, just a week ago, to
   the Cleveland Art Museum.
In accordance with Park School's tradition,
   the Sixth Grade herewith presents
its Report on this first comprehensive
   exhibit in the Mid-West
of what the museum catalog calls
   meditative creations
and the Cleveland *Plain Dealer* classifies
   as Monochromatic Art.
Whatever it was, there was lots of it:
   in room after immense room
of the museum's second story, walls
   were literally *papered*,
it's tempting to say, yes: wallpapered

with oblong or sometimes with
round or even triangular shapes, each
painted (or possibly stained)
One Color, and since these "shapes" were painted
(or stained) by well over one
hundred artists! men and women alike,
there were inevitably
—"alike" being the operative word—
duplications among these
monochromes . . . Let's say there were a number
of choice surfaces all too
synonymous with someone else's choice.
Who could tell *his* orange square
from *her* orange square when there was nothing
except poor orange itself
to constitute a square? Over the door
of the Museum, someone
named Rauschenberg had left his odd device:
a canvas is never empty—
isn't that the same as being never
full, or being always full?
Truth is, the Sixth Grade hasn't much to say

for Monochromes, even if
artists the world over are making them—
who could even pronounce their
names accordingly—from Kuwayama
to Jeroën de Rijke,
proceeding East to West, with Yves Klein and
Glenn Ligon intervening . . .
What *can* be said is that almost all those
prophylactic surfaces
seem to have lost their nerve after the first
application, as if paint
(if it was paint) could take us no further
than a glamorous veneer
which keeps anything else from happening.
Mrs. Eynon, you yourself
told us—we all remember what you said
that day in class (Joan Sturgess
even kept notes) about not starting out
too neat, too clean—as if each
initial gesture was obliged to be
a finishing touch! You said
an artist ought to leave—no, to *make*—room

for something to happen, not
to keep it from happening. You then said
that art was no accident,
but that it *was* interior as an
experience, and therefore,
if it *did* come from inside, from a place
not to be reached, only *reaching*,
it has to work itself *out*, which was likely
to be pretty messy, or
at least . . . not pretty. Well, in that whole show,
every single one of those
perfected monochromatic subjects
was arranged so that nothing
was likely to happen in them—they weren't
perfect, of course, they were just
clean. Isn't it weird that a museum
could even *find* a hundred
artists scared to death of getting dirty?
Who'd think of selling such things?
What price could be asked for such refusals
of life—such *undertakings?*
What the Sixth-Grade Spring-Trip Report very

specifically desires

is to be *overtaken* . . . So we left

that museum sooner than

later—what we really wanted to see

was authentic images

of Naked People (to be had elsewhere),

being deceived by so much

veil and cloud and mist and screen—so much

integument rather than

the needed figures . . . new mortalities.

* * * * * * * * * * * *

A REMONSTRANCE

Dear Mrs. Masters, by now

you've probably had a chance to look at

the Report on our spring-trip visit to

that Monochrome Exhibit

at the Cleveland Museum of Art, but

on the bus-ride home Something Happened

which we decided not to

discuss "officially", preferring to make
an informal statement you can deal with
  or ignore as you think best.
Of course you know that for this entire term
the Sixth Grade has had a guest student from
  Pretoria: Cal Gibney,
whose parents were killed last September
in a political riot, and whose
  surviving relatives sent
Cal to the States for security. During
all these months at Park School, Cal has become
  the most indispensable
member of the Sixth Grade Class. Even though,
or maybe just because, he is our one
  black Sixth-Grader (who also
possesses a super British accent),
Cal is always chosen to be our most
  "representative" student
—not even Duncan Chu has as many
linguistic advantages as Calvin,
  that's how we see it—so when,
on the bus-ride home from those Monochromes,

Mrs. Eynon asked someone to read us
　　　the international list
of artists whose work we had just seen, Cal
was our usual, our obvious choice
　　　and effectively ploughed through
the daunting roll of names without a hitch.
That's when it happened: Mrs. Eynon said
　　　"Thank you, Calvin, you did that
better than anyone else on this bus.
If I closed my eyes while you recited
　　　the world's monochrome artists,
I'd actually believe you were white . . ."
Nobody spoke another word until
　　　we were back at Park School. And
what word then? Mrs. Eynon had taught us
Space and Time, Composition and Color,
　　　but what about Black and White?

A CLASS PREDICAMENT

Dear Eddie Kass, even though
we're now the *Sixth*-Grade Class of course, no one's
forgotten you just because you left Park School
    in *Fifth* Grade. And Miss Husband
    told us (in Circle! which means
it *counts*) that our best way of showing how well
we remember you and your special way of
    "healing" people's hurt feelings
    would be to ask, even by
long distance, for your help the way we used to.
Like that time the Park School *News* sent Duncan Chu
    to interview the first black
    Mayor of Sandusky, who
told Duncan to his face that he was the first
Chink he had ever allowed into his house,
    and just repeating those words
    Duncan Chu broke down and cried
in Circle! But then you made us all (even
Duncan) laugh by saying that was the first chink

in the Mayor's armor as
an Elected Official.
So now we're writing this to the new address
Miss Husband asked the Office to find for you
down in North Carolina.
Of course everything depends
on your remembering that Circle is
our first Monday period, spent discussing
people's *personal* problems—
the kind that are different
from the problems we run into *as a Class* . . .
Well, last Monday, Miss Husband asked Jeunesse Ames
(you've *got to* remember *her*
on account of her weird name)
what she'd like to be, *after college*. Which was
a really funny question to ask Jeunesse!
Miss Husband *ought* to have said
"when you're grown up." Even so,
what could *either* College *or* Growing Up mean
to Jeunesse? If you remember her at all
you'll know the answer to that.
Besides, the whole Class—at least

all the *girls*, as well as Kenny Klein

who always knows what everyone wants to say

when it's their turn in Circle

(Kenny never says a *thing*)—

was waiting for what happened when Jeunesse said

what we all knew she would say. And she said it:

"I want to be a Doctor."

And Miss Husband said "Bravo!"

and stuff about its being so heroic,

even today, for women to be Doctors.

That was when Kenny Klein smiled

and sort of *coached* Miss Husband:

"Ask why." "Yes, tell us, Jeunesse, why *do* you want

to be a doctor." And Jeunesse said right away:

"So I get to see lots of

naked people all the time."

Even though we all guessed what she would say,

that *was* sort of a bombshell, and Miss Husband

got upset and said we all knew

Doctors weren't like that at all,

"Yes they *are*," Jeunesse said (now *she* was upset),

"My father's a doctor and I know they are."

Then Miss Husband laughed: she had
got over being upset,
and asked, "Do all the rest of you want to see
lots of naked people all the time?" Silence.
"All right, we'll take a vote by
secret ballot, even if
we don't have a proper booth to vote in. So
put your heads down on your desks and close your eyes.
Now I want you to cast your
vote by raising your right hands.
All those who would like to see naked people
vote first." We voted. And as it turned out,
even though the ballot was
"secret", the entire Sixth Grade
voted unanimously in favor of
seeing lots of naked people (Jeunesse peeked),
nobody for Miss Husband's
second choice. So then she got
upset again and said today's Circle was
over, and we should go to Miss Eynon's class
—we always have art Mondays—
"and perhaps, if you're lucky,

you'll get to look long enough at somebody
naked to learn something." She was really mad.
     Which is the real reason why
          we're writing: we can't go through
the rest of Sixth Grade with Miss Husband being
mad at us all the time just because we were
          honest about seeing naked
          people (if we had the chance).
Could you write to Kenny Klein here at Park School
before Circle next Monday with some advice?
     Miss Husband herself urged us
          to write, so we're positive
you'll think of a way out of this . . . For one thing,
all of us just *know* you'd have voted with us:
          that shows we remember you
          accurately, doesn't it?
The whole class sends our best wishes as well as
our hopes for a solution to our problem.

     Michael Hopkinson, Jeunesse
     Ames, Lois Hexter, Judy

Anders, Nancy Angrush, David Hammerstein, Lucy Wenzel, Kenneth & Jonathan Klein, Duncan Chu, Jane McCullough, Joan Sturgess, *both Arthur Engelhurst and David McConnehey were absent from school today.*

DEBATABLE QUESTIONS

Dear Mr. Lee,

It's true you told us,

when the School Year began, to call you Dinny

and we do—in class. But this is our first

chance to write an actual *letter*,

and now that the School Year is turning over,

it seems peculiar to be calling you

"Dinny" instead of "Mr. Lee" in

the *salutation*, which Miss Husband tells us

is how a formal letter should begin,

complemented at the other end

by a *valediction* (we'll deal with that part

whenever we get there). As it happens,

only half of our class (just the boys)

is (are?) writing this letter: in a course like

Social Studies, the girls seemed to find it

easier to ask "Dinny" (*Daddy?*)

questions than "Mr. Lee." Have you noticed that

boys prefer asking questions with no girls

present at all? The kind of questions
boys want answered in your Social Studies class
can be asked a lot more effortlessly
once it's understood that they'd be raised
exclusively in what might be reckoned as
the Company of Men. For example:
how much is owed to Society,
how much to Self-Respect, and how much to what
our mothers (not our fathers!) have taught us
about flushed or unflushed urinals?
How social an activity *is* flushing?
Arthur Engelhurst claims (*he would, of course*)
that leaving his pee in urinals
is a demonstration of selfhood, a kind
of creative presence (*not his words*).
He's got a point of view, except that
viewing it would be the least of our problems.
Arthur probably feels that if you flush
yourself away, you might not exist . . .
In museums, in railway-stations, and in
movie-theaters nowadays, it's all
automatic: you just step back, and

boom! or maybe *whoosh*! after which who could
          begin to recognize the contempt some men
            have for themselves and for all of us?
It's not as if there was a choice—pulling one
        one lever or another, like voting—
              it's all or nothing now, or just
nothing. Because our manners are made for us
        by machines, they're not, not really, manners
              any more . . . Manners must be man-made . . .
Flushing! the word itself is a clue: after all,
      we can flush with our faces as well as
            with our toilets (some people don't flush
at all—like dogs!—and others can't seem to stop:
        they're not flushing, they're *flush*!), and by the way,
              Duncan Chu says there's a suburb of
New York City called *Flushing Meadows*: just think,
      a whole field doing nothing but flushing,
            and people actually live there!
You know, Mr. Lee, now that we've written you
      most of our letter on Hamlet's problem:
            "To Flush or Not to Flush" (*just kidding*),
it seems less peculiar to talk about it

than we first thought—could the girls in our class
have something to contribute? Maybe
next week we could all learn together, though some
(boys) believe that a Standing Posture *has*
to have a lot (everything) to do
with *attitude*, especially on *voiding*
occasions. Looking forward, therefore, to
next week's classes,
(signed)
Yours Faithfully,
Kenneth & Jonathan Klein, David McConnehey,
Michael Hopkinson, Duncan Chu, David
Stackover. Please Note: Arthur
Engelhurst would not sign this letter, yet refused
to let us delete his name occurring
therein.
Apologies from the boys.

A THANK-YOU LETTER AND BEYOND

March 27th

Dear Eddie Kass,

We're back now for a second helping of your

generous brain, which may require some background:

dollars to doughnuts you'll remember

Nancy Angrush, our bright but bashful Classmate.

For once in her life Nancy showed spunk—about

you. Remember how shy she was? Though

we all knew she was the smartest girl in Class,

no one could make her talk during *Palaver*

(a word *she* didn't need to look up):

Palaver's our new name for *Circle*, chosen

last term because it sounded more . . . *serious*

for Monday Morning Reviews. It was

Duncan Chu's idea. Weren't you still at Park School

when he came up with those awful tongue-twisters

he insisted were "Late Latin Terms"?

If you were, you'll remember the response when

we tried one of them out—it happened to be

Palaver, and everyone agreed

it sounded a lot less feeble than *Circle*

for Monday-morning talks—we'll use *Palaver*

        till we find out what people forget

and what they remember. Anyhow, Eddie,

your fan Nancy Angrush, as you might expect,

        was determined you'd be on our side,

even when *yours* was in North Carolina.

She reminded us this wasn't the first time

        you'd come to our rescue, so of course

it was obvious we'd turn to you again,

if only by mail. Nancy foresaw that once

        Jeunesse Ames divulged her Awful Truth,

Miss Husband would insist on grilling us all

about our "futures". We voted: did we share

        the same interests (if not the same

motives) as our Jeunesse? Well, frankly, we did.

So Miss Husband had no case, though it was clear

        (from her Unforeseen but Distinct Tears)

that we were now facing a severe case of

Hurt Feelings. Once we'd *progressively voted*—

        Eddie, did you ever notice that

just by adding that adverb to any verb
used at our Park School, it would make whatever
           goes on around here sound ever so
democratic and therefore *enlightened?*—well,
having Progressively Voted and let One
           Voice speak for us all, *then*, Eddie dear,
once you make your Creative Response to this
new old play Jeunesse has so opportunely
           bestowed upon us this time around,
no one's feelings, not even Miss Husband's, will
be hurt. What you need to do now is to find
           —which in your case means to invent—
an appropriate sequel to what, these days,
we reverently proclaim, among ourselves,
           "Eddie Kass's Shocking Stocking Trick."
Whatever this letter becomes, it must first
be the True Expression of our Endless Thanks . . .
           All of us now understand that Our
Problem began when Jeunesse Ames was "compelled"
to clarify, in our Monday *Palaver*,
           why it was she *wanted* to grow up.
Eddie, have you the faintest idea how

many "adults" *share* Mr. J. M. Barrie's
life-long *unwillingness* to grow up?
Once Miss H started reading us *Peter Pan*,
we *hated* the thought of kids the world over
not just *not wanting* to grow up, but
actually *refusing* to. Then Miss H
got so pissed by what she called our attitude
to "her" *Peter Pan*, she resolved to
make each of us explain his or her "concept",
starting naturally with Miss Jeunesse Ames
during one of our next *Palavers* . . .
Of course you remember Jeunesse's "desire
to be a doctor": when Miss Husband called it
"a fine career, but a hard life for
an artistic, sensitive girl to select".
Whereupon that very same Sensitive Girl
pointed out that it was her best chance
to see people naked. Then Miss Husband—not
at all convinced when Jeunesse went on to say
"*everybody I know* wants to see
people naked"—deemed the Class needed to vote,
which would determine if naked was truly

how we all "wanted to see people" . . .
Then Arthur Engelhurst, who habitually
spurns voting with our Class on those *issues* which
          Park School surmises must (and by votes!)
reach a Proper End—Arthur voted. Thereby
the Class voted *unanimously*, and the sole
          hurt feelings were Miss Husband's. Eddie,
wouldn't that have shocked you? That our famously
"unshockable" teacher would have reacted
          to a truly unanimous vote
so . . . *shockingly*? So we put Kass on the case,
and you saw exactly what had to be done.

          Of course we were scrupulous about
following your directions—followed them to
the letter (it was exciting that they were
          the opposite of any "letter"
you'd have made us write). It was with absolute
(if astonished) conviction that we saw *this*
          was just what the doctor had ordered.
As if you knew, before our letter arrived,
what must be done, and how, when, and where we must
          do it, making clear how the weird plot

had to work. But the mystery is how *you*
could have known what to do from the beginning.

It all worked just as you said it would,
once Miss Husband managed to get our—or by then,
to get *her*—present open: you insisted
it had to be received as a Peace
Offering—"propitiatory" you said.
She began by gasping, then giggling a bit too
loud, then devotionally swearing
she had never owned even a *single pair* of
Black Fishnet Stockings in her life! Had never
dreamed of buying such things for *herself,*
though now, thanks to us, she actually *owned*
six pairs of what must be (mouthing the words with
an emphasis both relishing and
reprimanding) "suitable wear for dancing
French *cancans* all night long at someone's wedding"
(*the* event all Park School was aware
would occur next June). By now Miss Husband was
laughing so helplessly we all knew she had
recovered from her irreverent
students' unanimous ballot: they *wanted*

to see people naked (given half a chance).

        All right, sir, you won that round. But now,
Eddie, *now* we're facing a quandary much
more serious than the one you so neatly
        solved for us: it was—at least it seemed—
easy for you to bestow that gift of six
pairs of Black Fishnet Stockings, a choice thought of
        by no one, not even by naughty
Jeunesse. Did someone say we faced a problem?
No problem! We'll just write Eddie Kass again.

        There's no help for it, at least there's no
other help, as the old man says in the old plays.
And then he tells you: "You may not recall, old friend,
        having eschewed our Park School customs,
that this year—Eddie, how could you forget?—this year
is Our Turn—doesn't it come back to you now?

        This year is our very own Sixth Grade's
turn, our chance to make what Mrs. Masters calls
a "suitable show" for our big-time Midwest
        Progressive Festival. Forgot that?
Then you'll never guess what comes next. Now hear this:
Miss Husband, ever alert for lapses in

Student Taste, proposes we perform
Our Town—these are her actual words—*"which might
well be about life and death right here in our
Sandusky."* We always recognize
that odd vibration when she wants us to think
she's on the verge of tears, implying something
like *"Our Town = your Sixth Grade,"* and
then, with terrible conviction, announcing
"You're in it!" entirely forgetting how much
we abhorred that wretched tear-jerker
the Cleveland Playhouse put on over Christmas
when "children could share it with their families
and find out how much there was in it
for them." You were here then, Eddie, you'll recall
our concerted response to *that* bright idea:
there are at least twenty roles—if we
Sixth Graders staged *Our Town*, each of us would be
playing at least two parts—and no one, Eddie,
could handle *that* except you (and you're
in Asheville now), and our own Jeunesse, of course,
who's acted (up) since babyhood, beginning
her stage career with a one-word speech:

"*giddy-ap*," likely syllables for a tot
(lucky Jeunesse: it's the curtain-line). We'll save
        all that for Later; for Now you must
realize—Eddie, it's vital you know who's
at the root of our troubles (if not the root,
        the most obvious branch): Jeunesse Ames
has grown up to *adore* the very play in which
what she spoke back then (and nearly all
        she *could* speak) was "*giddy-ap*." That play
happens to be *Woyzeck* (also spelled *Wozzeck*)—
you never heard of it, Eddie, no one has
        (that's why there's a second spelling);
the author was a German named Büchner who died
in 1836, about ten years older than any of us,
        and no one ever heard of the dude
till *another* Kraut named Berg—Alban Berg—turned
his forsaken fragment into an *opera*
        (spelled *Wozzeck*) in 1925.
The spelling doesn't count—we weren't even born
back then. But here's what does count for us, Eddie:
        the best actress in Park School (guess who)
read *Woyzeck* to us—not *Peter Pan*, *Woyzeck*!

and now the Sixth Grade longs to perform this great
fragment for the Midwest Progressive
Festival, of course. We love this play, Eddie,
because as soon as Jeunesse read it to us
we realized it was the first script
we've encountered at Park School that's not deadly—
that doesn't lead to death: *death just isn't in it*!
and get this, Eddie, there's no
S.I. either (surely you haven't forgotten S.I.
—*Sexual Intercourse*—just because you're in
North Carolina now instead of
concupiscent Ohio, have you, Eddie?).
We all want to see a play which doesn't lead
to death or even endorse S.I.
(we were amazed when Jeunesse read us *Woyzeck*
that first time), but we don't see how we can
convince Miss Husband, who certainly
never heard of the play, added to the fact that it's
Jeunesse, our top Büchner fan, who just happens
to be Park School's top nudity fan . . .
So we're back, Eddie. After Fishnet Stockings,
half the Class believes we—you—have a good chance,

but the rest feel our *best* chance is for
you, Eddie, to explain to our suspicious
teacher (who so often suspects the worst of *us*)
    that since this entire text consists of
fragments (scenes staged in any order that suits
whatever talents we find amongst ourselves),
    the play *Woyzeck* is best suited for
unseasoned performers like our Sixth-Grade selves.
Once Jeunesse read us the play and we could make
    our own copies and begin to fit
ourselves into whatever scenes . . . work for us,
weren't we just as likely as Jeunesse to make
    this experiment suit the public
Mrs. Masters is likely to snag for us.
That much we know, though haven't we come to feel
    Jeunesse is our star, and if we give
several performances, Jeunesse would be
Marie in all of them . . . As she's often said:
    Woyzeck was my horsie from the first.

*   *   *   *   *   *   *   *   *   *   *   *   *   *

April 1st (Fools' Day) Dear Eddie Kass,
As sternly as such news can be imparted,
we've just been told we have no chance to perform
Woyzeck here, or anywhere else in
the USA. It seems that our age, or our
lack of age, is against us, as always
        when *real*—money-making—performers
are the competition. Those Royal Canadians promptly
invited "our" Jeunesse, first as a mascot
        but soon afterwards as a child star
in their productions (we have, and wish to have,
no notion of her underhand participation
        in such . . . manipulations). The Class
continues its work, *i.e.* toward Seventh Grade,
which means for most of us, most of the time, what
        we have always intended. After
so much *voting*, a let-down for all of us,
of course, but Mrs. Masters and Dinny Lee
        (surely you'll remember the latter)
have been very careful to keep us on our
true course, as Miss Husband calls it, and perhaps
        you can get up here, not of course for

Jeunesse in *Woyzeck,* but at least for what our
Class decides to do for the damn *Festival;*
　　　　　palpably it will not be *Our Town,*
but (Nancy Angrush keen on this) *another*
Wilder play called *The Skin of Our Teeth*—Wilder
　　　　　himself says: *It comes alive under*
conditions of crisis. Doesn't that sound like
the sort of show we should get ourselves into?
　　　　　Eddie, read it yourself: dinosaurs
in Act 1 and things like that you're sure to love.
We're all eager to have you with us, any role
　　　　　you fancy, as long as it's under
conditions of crisis. Looking over this
shocking piece of negativity, it's clear
　　　　　we mustn't be quite so stiff around
the upper lip. Fancy our horror to learn
from originals stuck to her typed ms
　　　　　(from which all of our copies were made)
that Jeunesse *rewrote the play*! S.I. appears
throughout (every page) and when Woyzeck
　　　　　murders Marie, *that* is the instant
her two-year-old child, doubtless a boy,

brings down the curtain to endless, innocent

        cries of *giddy-ap*! (do we suppose

baby Jeunesse took it all in?). Great fun to

imagine the recoil of Masters, Husband

        and Co., not to mention varying

satisfactions of Jeunesse Ames, if she had

thoughts for the likes of us in her new career . . .

        All of us send you what all of us

hope is our best love from a reduced Sixth Grade,

though hopefully wiser when we soon become

        Park School's no longer savaged Seventh.

WHAT SHE TAUGHT US

Herein is Revealed what our
Miss Husband sought & perhaps
succeeded in Imparting to her Charges:
the unknown and unsuspected Merits
—and defects too—of Oysters and Oystering.

*

Dear Class, that Spring weekend—a tight fit
    for those three days when Charles—*Charles*
    who? Why, Charles Jonas, of course,
my own Charles, who showed me the way to this
bleak yet blessed coast for my first "oyster weekend"
—did none of you recall his name (which will soon
be mine, yes, next year—no, *next month*! you'll
    call me Mrs. Jonas, but till then,
    you still have one good thing
to learn from *Miss Husband*: I'm quite sure
none of you has had—not here in these Midwest
wastelands (you know what I mean: Ohio is nice

but no *native* there can even suggest

a real oyster *collation,*

from gathering to serving

to consumption). Let me try though, maybe I have

some vestige of the shore about me still, enough

to make you want to try it yourselves. See here:

we'll let the oysters lead. Follow the leader . . .

Dear Class: daily or all day

it rains hard in the Hamptons,

at least in April (when I'm there), so we go

about our oystering chores somewhat wetter

than we would prefer, yet go we must. Goodness!

what a mess we are—even the oysters: so

secretive, at least till lunch;

anything that's swallowed whole

is unlikely to remain a mystery

for long. As for the Moment of Truth, I guess

what's gastronomic has a veracity

unique among human experiences.

Yet how relentlessly these

creatures spurn solicitude!

Sealed, annealed, utterly brainless, and for all

their shared beds, as Dickens observed, "separate
to the end," their message disdains all of us:
there's more than one way to yield. Of which merely
the crassest—soonest undone—
is that we must first rip them
free of their rocks (their bed-rocks, just so), even
as the stinking, sawing sedge sucks them under
black mud swarming with hermit-crabs swathed in their
pilfered snail-shells, the distraught minnows swiftly
dissolving like obsessions,
the crazed surf shambling away,
and whatever power life grants the oysters
holding on, holding out for dear . . . life. Often
the stones give way first, before *they* will, but
still we gather them, goodness yes, we keep at
our oystering for dear life
too, gathering enough of
the poor, astonishingly silent victims
for whatever repast the present proposes,
even if our hands are bloody as meat—for
a luncheon Queen Victoria preferred: "Two
barrels of Wellfleet Oysters,

points down" could last across
the ocean, all the way to Windsor, wakening
a widow's taste. We ate them one noontime,
fresh out of their helpless armor which had been
so formidably grooved (though it proved our own
    equally helpless human
    reversal wiser still: *keep*
the bones and stones inside, never leave the sea.
"He was a brave man," Swift said, "who first et one."
Even now, the precedent of centuries
is not always enough. Impelling the knife
    into muscles that mold valves
    so close to being impartial,
the surrender, when it comes—and it *must* come,
lavish after that first grudging release back
there in the sea, the giving-over, this time,
of despair—makes me reflect to some purpose:
    like Oscar and the oysters
    I feel "always a little
immortal when in the sea." What happens, now
we are out? Is the risk worth taking for a
potential pearl? No, what we're really after

is that moment of recess, the turn and tear

    of the blade that, tightening,

    tortures, ultimately tells.

When you spread the shells, something always sticks to

the wrong one, and some few cold drops of ichor

dribble into the sand: in the full half shell,

as well as a Fautrier, a Zen garden,

    and the smell of herring-brine

    that Ferenczi insisted

we remember from the womb, Lunch Is Served

in shiny stoneware sockets, ultramarine

milk in the sea's freshest, filthiest chalice.

More easily an emblem for the Inner

    Man than dinner, sundered, for

    his stomach. We swallow them

queasily, never really savoring what

we promised to taste so conscientiously,

wondering as we gulp when it is—back then?

or now? or maybe tomorrow?—that they're dead.

    Unless they're alive in us,

    and we're just extant oysters.

                *

Well, Miss Husband, or Mrs. Jonas (we have
other names for you too, but we're keeping them
    for ourselves). What we won't keep
        is our *regalement* of What
you do for the Oysters, or is it What they
do for You? And our gratification that
you understand the word-games we're all learning
to play. Of course the entire class is flattered
    (especially those three girls
        who won't give their names, although
they insist you know who they are)—flattered by
your *awareness* of our efforts—"regalement,"
nine lines back, is typical—to speak the same
language you do, so to speak. Our thanks for that,
        for "Oysters and Oystering"
        and most of all *for you*, dear
Miss Husband, or, taking a prelusive step,
dear Mrs. Jonas, from
                your old Sixth Grade Class,
prelusively the Seventh Grade of Park School.

                                    2000

                    *

Wherein was also shown the rare Covenant
of Utterance uniting
our cherished Schoolmarm with her
prankish Sixth Graders: a passionate, a life-
transforming Participation of the Tongue,
a shared response to all that Words express,
moving toward unforeseen challenges and risks
with a confidence our education has inspired.

DINNY LEE EXPLAINS

Boys and Girls . . . I always call you that,
don't I? What other names could I use?
But you know as well as I do that here,

right here at Park, which (as schools go)
is a pretty enlightened institution,
there happen to be some individuals

who refer to themselves as *teachers* just like
your Miss Husband and like me, yet who prefer
using more inflated forms of address for

boys and girls. I suspect that you noticed this
propensity of these individuals
right away, probably sooner than I did,

and frankly, it seems to me that in a school
as enlightened as Park, where our "assignment"
(to employ a scholastic term if I may)

is to treat *learning* as an event valued
for itself and not to be upgraded by
declaring our students are superior

to mere *boys & girls* . . . Well, I'm certain you see
what I'm getting at—it comes down or maybe
comes up to getting every one of us,

teachers *and* students alike, off on the wrong . . .
foot or hand, in any case on the wrong heart!
Isn't that what it is we do whenever

we address our youngsters, sumptuously or
not, as *Ladies & Gentlemen?* whenever
we direct our classes of boys and girls

to the rest-rooms for *ladies and gentlemen* . . .
That's surely not how the system we're trying
to live by operates . . . Whenever I hear

Mrs. Masters "flattering" her dear Sixth Grade
—*contractually* mine as much as hers—
as "*my esteemed Ladies & Gentlemen*"

I want to play hooky. If you can't be addressed
as *Boys & Girls* when you're in Sixth Grade
then I can't help believing we've been barking

up the wrong tree. Meanwhile, our friend Miss Husband
(who in spite of her curious maiden name
is no gentleman—she's not even *married!*)

has asked me to defend or at least to justify her
favorite book, now subject to your disfavor.
It seems despite the talent of my colleague's

admired rest-period readings, on this go-round
her much-admired rendition of *Peter Pan
or The Boy Who Would Not Grow Up*

was roundly reproved by your Sixth Grade,
indeed rejected by Girls as well as Boys,
the latter, I gather, having no sympathy even

for the subsequent title *PP and the Lost Boys*
(as Peter himself would call them, his own
more plaintive monicker being *The Lost Piper*),

while the Girls' disapprobation seems to afford
no tolerance for odd ducks, stray dogs, maybe even
queer fish and surely no dumb bunnies, though

one thing I now know, after less than two weeks'
Rest-Period exposure to Miss Husband's reading,
is that you have lost all patience for PP,

which an equally dubious James Barrie
offered in 1903 as ANON: A CLOSED BOOK,
refusing to see it printed as a *play* till 1928,

after all three prompt-scripts of 1903, -04 and -05
were published six years later as a *novel*
(which Barrie in 1920 hopefully transformed

for Paramount into a screenplay for Chaplin
who hated the damn thing, though Mr. Disney,
in another thirty years, would have no doubts

of its filmic possibilities) and now, after
what I'm sure was Miss Husband's finest
Rest-Period version, she sourly complains,

(and perhaps with just cause) that the entire
Sixth Grade of Park School has promptly
developed an identical and permanent distaste

for *The Boy Who Would Not Grow Up* and for
all his playmates, friends and foes, including
the notorious and appropriately sinister

Captain Hook—I myself readily accept, in fact
even share some sentiment for Captain Hook,
though I just can't stand Tinker-Bell, for whom

I always refused to admit I believed in fairies,
and nursed a vague larger distaste for the whole
business Miss Husband has chosen to perform

for your delectation. I'm not disputing
her choice, and God knows I'm not disputing
yours, but poor Alberta was so jarred by your

reaction that she's asked me to "speak to you."
I'm sure you understand that she really wants
to continue with *Peter Pan*, which she loves,

but now suspects she needs (or maybe *you* need)
some sort of . . . negotiation (that's her word,
I'm sure you recognize it). I'd dearly love

to oblige Alberta (and perhaps the Sixth Grade
as well). For instance, do you people realize
that since its first performance (in 1904)

PP has been the most popular play in the English-
speaking world? It wasn't even a play when Barrie
first wrote it! Reason enough to examine

not just the text but your distaste for the text
despite official approval: it's worth learning
why *anything*—even *Peter Pan*—is capable of

being a "universal success", though you yourselves
may be prepared, by the last ten lines, to vomit,
assuming you haven't already puked your hearts out

in medias res. You remember that the first thing
Peter says to Wendy is "No one ever touches me."
And remains forever disembodied—not so much

a myth as a sublime object. As you see from Alberta's
distress, *Peter Pan* stands in our culture as a monument
to the impossibility of its own class: represents

the child, speaks to and for children, addresses them
as a group existing for the book, much as the book
exists for them. But *Peter Pan* has never been a book

for children at all! All such fictions (think of
Alice in Wonderland) paint the child as outsider
to his own process, then aims, quite shamelessly,

to take the child in. Look, Boys and Girls, *Peter Pan*
was not meant for children. It first appeared
in a novel for adults. Barrie's 1902 story,

The Little White Bird, is told to a little boy
whom the narrator is trying to steal. To become
"a work for children" it was stripped from its source,

transformed into a play, and sent out on its own.
The idea that childhood is *something separate*
which can be scrutinized and assessed makes

children something which grown-ups have simply ceased to be. Which you have discovered, but every adult who loves *PP* will never forgive you for this

discovery. Barrie later made his sole attempt to write his book as a *story for children*. Alas, *PP* was a childen's classic before it was

a children's book. Barrie's attempt to reclaim *PP* (he called it *Peter Pan & Wendy*) was a failure. By 1911 *PP* was already

such an acclaimed phenomenon that Barrie himself could only intervene back into its history *from outside*. Of course *PP & W*

failed. *Peter Pan* went on without it. Could *only* go on without it because it had come to signify an innocence, a simplicity which every line of

Barrie's 1911 text belies. As you can tell from the first line of that 1911 story: "All children, except one, grow up." However, Boys and Girls,

it's your success (growing up, God save us) which
upsets Miss Husband and other grownups who
prefer themselves (and you) to fail. I'm sorry

to torment you with all these versions and dates,
which I know bore you. But I think I've given you
a way of hearing Miss Husband read *PP*

which will both mollify you and placate her.
Just remember what you already know but
may not understand: people who "love *PP*"

have ignored the fact that presenting the Child
as Innocent is not the same thing as repressing
the Child's sexuality—it is, always, holding off

any possible challenge to their own. I'll try to
join you after lunch tomorrow when Miss H
performs. Maybe we can exchange winks . . . Or not.

E PLURIBUS UNUM

This, dear Miss Husband,
is our Class Poem
composed in your honor and, we hope,
clearly reflecting your image as
a bright particular star
in the pedagogical
constellation of our dear Park School.
All year long you have *coruscated*
with a signal meaning for the twelve of us
who rely upon your . . . radiance. Writing
this poem together, our
Sixth Grade Class has discovered
by degrees, each of us for ourselves,
that *Progressive Education* works
by confidence in
what the Founders called
"mutual stimulus"—nowadays
most students tend to call it "teamwork"—
but regardless what it's called
by us now or by them then,

the spirit of *collaboration* kept us
pecking keenly for the seeds you had scattered,
  along with those we unearthed
  in the Park School Library.
That was where you had "exiled" our class
"for *context*," though we longed to inspect
  your *own* books (we had
  spied those same volumes
chez nous, though our parents seemed averse
to our switching them from home shelves to
  locations where we might "read
  them for ourselves"). Miss Husband
wasn't the least bit averse about *her* books
and always lent them to us, no questions asked.
  Then there were those other joys:
  scarlet capes, even leather ones
anyone could wear if he or she
remained within the bounds of Park School,
  and for the timid,
  entrée was granted
to that big wire cage behind your desk
with its docile flock of plump ring-doves
  to be hugged and held cooing

on our laps for the whole class . . .
Even so, Miss Husband, you *did* exile us
(half-way through the second volume of *Alice*)
from your Enchanted Classroom to find
what we would have to *disinter* from
the Park School Library stacks
(not exactly *interred* there,
but it seemed we had to dig awfully deep
for what we didn't know we were looking for).
Maybe that's the true allure
of libraries—lighting on
a proper author's scandalous life
right next to the official version.
That's just what happened
(post *Alice*) last week,
so of course that's what our Class Poem
must now become: a "library find"
bestowed on Miss Husband as
a sign of our understanding . . .
Not a put-down of *Alice*'s creator,
but an indication that within each life,
even the most seemingly

respectable and even

virtuous life, there must be some form

of the Destructive Impulse, some

inexplicable

nastiness—call it

the Human Touch—and our class found it

in an edition of old letters . . .

All this year, Mr. Lee (alias Dinny,

the science teacher who takes our class on trips)

kept "reassuring" us that

a true Creative Result

was much likelier to be produced

by the meeting of *twelve minds* than by

some solitary

genius, and he's right!

Somehow he must have known. Composing

this year's Class Poem (these homely lines

in your honor, Miss Husband)

has been almost easily

"created" by our *combined* sedulousness,

even if the twelve of us produce verses

so blank they need to be nursed

(or even doctored) by some
outsider's welcome endowment of
individual inspiration,
    if such things exist,
    as we now believe:
our rest-period readings have proved
that nothing could be more *inspired*, more
    individual than listening
    to *Alice in Wonderland*
and then to *Alice through the Looking-Glass*—both
of which Miss Husband has duly daily read.
    Most of our Class had never
    read either book, and only
three of us (all girls) had had *lections*,
which *sounds* like a contagious disease,
    shingles or *measles*,
    but Miss Husband says
it means *Scripture recited*. She claims
that family readings of *Alice*
    have become tantamount to
    bygone Biblical sessions
and declared herself "appalled" that most of us

were ignorant of Alice and her new friends,
though *enemies* seems a more
accurate term, once that girl
got herself down the rabbit-hole—got
herself *underground*, to use Mr. Carroll's
more ghoulish title
for where she got to—
Alice's Adventures Underground,
scarcely *our* notion of Wonderland . . .
Luckily a whole month more
of rest-period readings
lies ahead, in which the finishing touches
of pseudo-scriptural consecration may
still apply and our *lections*
persist through *The Looking-Glass.*
Though aggrieved, Miss Husband is eager
for us to get to know not only
shape-shifting Alice
but that huge troupe of
savage nitwits, screaming duchesses,
grinning cats, loveless old men mumbling
what *some critics* call "surreal

parodies of stale pastorals";
nobody kind, not even Talking Flowers,
and Alice herself, class-starched, annoyed to be
mistaken for a *servant* . . .
But even before we were
half-way through *Wonderland*, there was lots
to look up in the library stacks
in pursuit of our
research assignment,
particularly when it concerned
Charles Dodgson *and* Lewis Carroll, who
appear quite "importunate"
(at least the former figure
about the latter one) about *not being*
the identical person, regardless of
the all-too-apparent facts.
Once we got into the stacks,
the subject for *our poem* became
equally apparent: all about
our affections for
the great writer and
our distaste for the *person* who just

happened to *be* that writer, the truth

we thereby *unearthed*, or its

effect on our characters,

on our lives *as readers*: that is the homage

we want to pay Miss Husband, what *this poem*

really seeks to represent.

The library stacks, as soon

as *Lewis Carroll* was named, sent us

to *Charles Dodgson* and to letters which

in *actual* life

proved there and then

(as opposed to his *fiction*, in which

friendly puppies frequently appear

on Wonderland's friendly lawns)

that Dodgson *did not like dogs*,

and when one attacked him on a visit to

Dean Liddell (whose daughter Alice had inspired

Alice), Charles Dodgson refused

ever to visit again

unless that dog was destroyed, sending

the Dean an exact diagram of

canine tooth-marks (and

in addition an

incontrovertible photograph

of his torn tweed trouser-leg!) And yet

Dodgson is said to have been

charming with, and charmed by,

(small) creatures, even to have treated them as

somewhat superior to human beings

whom they, in whimsy, either

represented or replaced.

Perhaps this might be, in addition,

the proper place for Lewis Carroll's

message to a child:

that he forgot what

the story of *Alice* was about,

"but I think it was about malice."

Remember, Dear Miss Husband,

it was from you we learned that

the man *Carroll* created a Calendar

of Saints, including a *White Knight*, a *Dormouse*,

a *Mock Turtle*, and

many apt Sinners,

yet that the man *Dodgson*, for

all his rules of symbolic logic,

was not much more than

a vengeful killer,

and that these *two characters* were *one*

and the same person! For which knowledge

our uneasy thanks and our

affectionate pupilage.

Unanimously signed by the entire Sixth Grade

in honor of our beloved

teacher Alberta Husband

Lucie Wenzel	Duncan Chu
Nancy Angrush	Arthur Engelhurst
Jeunesse Ames	David Hammerstein
Anne Wobie	David Stackover
Jane McCullough	David McConnehey
Joan Sturgess	Kenneth Klein

the authors thereof

A COMMUNICATION
FROM MRS. MASTERS

My dear Sixth Graders, good morning!

I take it you'd cringe at the prospect of your
misguided Principal addressing you as
dear Girls & Boys, or

as the more often (and less politely) heard
dear Boys & Girls. Might you not flinch worse still
if I harangued you

on my unrehearsed drop-in as *dear Ladies
& Gentlemen*? I shall not try your patience
further on this visit . . .

My dear Sixth Graders, as you briefly remain,

You have been so plucky, during the school year,
writing to me whenever stressful events
occur that press you

to protest or simply to discuss, in hopes
of any relief I might afford you, that
I am happy to

offer what comfort I can: Virtually
all your complaints, or let us call them merely
the confusions spun

so frankly and fastidiously as you have
set them before me (yet, as I hear them, so
eloquently put),

strike me as merely *situational*, derived
(if I interpret your strain accurately)
from crises confined

to what I should categorize as merely
Sixth-Grade predicaments which by now you twelve,
perhaps with my help,'

have thoroughly understood and so mastered
that I can assure you that the difficulties
you confront next year,

and in all the Park School years to come, will be,
in their new manifestations, no simpler
or, let's say, no less

difficult than those you have by now found quite
comfortable from familiarity.
Hence I am eager

to welcome you to the Seventh Grade, which I can
assure you will be altogether other,
quite unfamiliar

and consequently, for some of you, perhaps
more to your disinclination, for others,
more to your liking.

I am quite unable to justify such
discrepancies, but you may be certain of
one thing—one prospect:

nothing will be *the same*, everything will be
altered for all of you, and therefore I am
prepared to receive

from every one of you those new messages
quite as astonishing, as dissuasive and as
confounding as my

fate has been hitherto—yet I shall not be
cowed, for no plight, I am thoroughly convinced,
will be capable

of deterring your Mrs. Masters beyond
past importunings. So, my dear young people,
let us together

enjoy the festivities of the season
and confront with equal wills and energies
those difficulties

and demands we shall all be sure to incur,
as we have incurred and *prevailed over* those
just now incurred.

I salute you, Sixth Graders as you have been
and Seventh Graders as you shall become, in my
true guise which is one

as I trust you know already, of concern,
of co-operation, and—never doubt it—
of our shared success.

Regina Masters

ACKNOWLEDGMENTS

"A Proposed Curriculum Change": *The Antioch Review*; *The Best American Poetry 2012*

"A Report, Followed by a Remonstrance": *The Antioch Review*

"Another Elucidation" and "Debatable Questions": *The Hopkins Review*

"E Pluribus Unum": *Parnassus*

"A Class Predicament": *Raritan*

"Back from Our Spring Trip," "Arthur Englander's Back in School," "A Fifth-Grade Protest," and "What the Future Has in Store": *Without Saying* (Turtle Point Press, 2008; as a group titled "School Days")